Earning Money through Crypto Currency Airdrops, Bounties, Faucets, Cloud Mining Websites and Exchanges

By

Dr. Hidaia Mahmood Alassouli

Hidaia_alassouli@hotmail.com

1. Introduction:

A crypto faucet is a website that will give you satoshis in exchange for viewing ads or completing simple tasks. Crypto currency mining is the process in which transactions between users are verified and added into the block chain. The process of mining is also responsible for introducing new coins into the existing circulating supply and is one of the key elements that allow cryptocurrencies to work as a peer-to-peer decentralized network, without the need for a third party central authority.

Cloud mining happens in the "cloud." That basically means that the hardware used for mining is not physically located at your premises, but it is accessed remotely through the internet.

An airdrop, in the cryptocurrency business, is a marketing stunt that involves sending free coins or tokens to wallet addresses in order to promote awareness of a new virtual currency.

In Bounty programs, participants get cryptocurrencies in exchange for promotion.

A cryptocurrency exchange is any system that operates on the basis of trading cryptocurrencies with other assets.

There are also some on-line service designed for those who wants to exchange electronic currencies quickly, safely and at a favorable rate, such as: Webmoney, Perfect Money, AdvCash, Payeer, Skrill, Neteller, Epay, Payza, PayPal, Visa/Master Card, Western union, MoneyGram, Bitcoin, Ethereum, Litecoin.

This work will guide the user to a list of online sources to earn money in the internet through crypto faucets, mining, cloud mining, airdrops and bounties. Then I will list some of the best online crypto currency exchanges and electronic currencies exchangers that can be used.

The book consists from the following parts:

1. Some sources for crypto faucets
2. Definition of cryptocurrency mining and cloud minining
3. Some useful websites for cryptocurrency mining and cloud minining
4. Airdrop and Bounty definitions
5. Some online sources to look for airdrops and bounties events
6. Some Youtube channels to fellow up latest airdrops, faucets and mining websites
7. Some websites to get information about cryptocurrency prices and market capitalization
8. Some trusted cryptocurrency exchanges
9. Some exchanger monitoring platforms
10. Some electronic currencies exchangers

2. Some sources for crypto faucets

A crypto faucet is a website that will give you satoshis in exchange for viewing ads or completing simple tasks. A satoshi is the smallest trading unit of a coin, worth 0.00000001 BTC in the case of BitCoin. Crypto faucets exist for most alt coins.

Crypto faucets are about as close as you can get to regularly getting coins for free. In a lot of cases you simply have to solve a captcha and collect your satoshis.

Here a list of some crypto faucets websites.

Note that some of these sites may be not active and closed now. I just gave sample of the websites that worked as faucets before publishing this book.

- https://faucethub.io
- https://faucetpay.io/
- https://www.eobot.com/faucet
- https://allcoins.pw
- https://h2ox.io/
- https://getzen.cash/
- https://gramfree.net/
- https://bitfortune.club/index
- https://www.kswallet.net/register
- https://lbry.tv/
- https://btcaptcha.com
- https://www.kswallet.net/register
- https://addash.cc-
- http://rub-coin.com/?i=67338
- http://bitco220.co/register.php
- http://multicoinfaucet.website/bch/
- https://phoneum.io
- https://game.trifoliumcoin.com
- https://trafficshout.com
- https://btcpop.co/
- https://moremoney.io/
- ttps://stakesx.io/platform/register.html
- https://litecoinads.com/
- https://www.hedgie.io/journey
- https://ad9t.com/register
- https://coinspot.fun/cs/index.php
- bitlucky.io/faucet
- http://xbit.co.in/faucet/

- http://worldofbitco.in
- https://btc4free.site/faucet :
- http://www.bitcoin-s.com/bitcoincash
- http://queenfaucet.website/bch
- http://www.8raa.com/bitcoincash/
- http://www.vivocoin.com/
- http://getfree.co.in
- https://bagi.co.in
- https://adbtc.top
- http://www.starbits.io
- http://timeforbitco.in/
- http://chronox.co.in/
- http://sunbtc.space/
- https://faucet.bitcoins43.com/
- http://freebitcoin.win/
- http://coindice.win
- http://coinpot.win
- www.gobits.io
- www.claimbits.io/
- https://btc4free.today/
- https://blackcoinfaucet.com/faucet-list/ has the faucet lists for all coins
- https://freedoge.co.in/
- https://coinfaucet.io/.
- https://earningbch.com/
- https://www.faucetcrypto.com/
- http://earnethers.com/
- http://ethxup.com/
- https://www.speedup-faucet.com/ether/index.php
- http://moonbit.co.in
- https://honeymoney.co.in/dashboard/:
- https://freebitco.in
- https://bitcoinker.com
- https://www.mybithouse.com/
- http://adbtc.top
- https://btcclicks.com/
- https://coinbulb.com
- http://getyourbitco.in/
- http://btcbox.in/
- http://dogebox.in/
- http://litebox.in/

- https://freebitco.in claim every hour.
- https://afreebitco.in/jxapobitcoinfaucet/ websites has all Xapo faucets
- EOT wallet https://eotwallet.com/ to earn eot coins.
- http://faucet.gay.money
- https://bitnyx.com/faucet.
- https://cointiply.com/faucet.
- https://blackcoinfaucet.com/faucet-list/ has the faucet lists for all coins
- https://freecardano.com/free
- https://www.airdrips.com/
- https://freedoge.co.in.
- In https://gamex.co.in
- http://fieldbitcoins.com/
- https://www.instant-btc.eu/en
- https://tradesatoshi.com/Faucet
- https://blackcoinfaucet.com/page/faucet
- https://panel.bither.one/getbither
- https://coinspot.fun/cs/index.php

3. Definition of cryptocurrency mining and cloud minining:

Crypto currency mining is the process in which transactions between users are verified and added into the block chain public ledger. The process of mining is also responsible for introducing new coins into the existing circulating supply and is one of the key elements that allow cryptocurrencies to work as a peer-to-peer decentralized network, without the need for a third party central authority.

Bitcoin is the most popular and well-established example of a mineable cryptocurrency, but it is worth noting that not all cryptocurrencies are mineable. Bitcoin mining is based on a consensus algorithm called Proof of Work.

 A miner is a node in the network that collects transactions and organizes them into blocks. Whenever transactions are made, all network nodes receive them and verify their validity. Then, miner nodes gather these transactions from the memory pool and begin assembling them into a block (candidate block).

The first step of mining a block is to individually hash each transaction taken from the memory pool, but before starting the process, the miner node adds a transaction where they send themselves the mining reward (block reward). This transaction is referred to as the coinbase transaction, which is a transaction where coins get created 'out of thin air' and, in most cases, is the first transaction to be recorded in a new block.

After every transaction is hashed, the hashes are then organized into something called a Merkle Tree (or a hash tree) - which is formed by organizing the various transaction hashes into pairs and then hashing them. The outputs are then organized into pairs and hashed once again, and the process is repeated until "the top of the tree" is reached. The top of the tree is also called a root hash (or Merkle root) and is basically a single hash that represents all the previous hashes that were used to generate it.

The root hash - along with the hash of the previous block and a random number called nonce - is then placed into the block's header. The block header is then hashed producing an output based on those elements (root hash, previous block's hash, and nonce) plus a few other parameters. The resulting output is the block hash and will serve as the identifier of the newly generated block (candidate block).

In order to be considered valid, the output (block hash) must be less than a certain target value that is determined by the protocol. In other words, the block hash must start with a certain number of zeros.

The target value - also known as the hashing difficulty - is regularly adjusted by the protocol, ensuring that the rate at which new blocks are created remains constant and proportional to the amount of hashing power devoted to the network.

Therefore, every time new miners join the network and competition increases, the hashing difficulty will raise, preventing the average block time from decreasing. In contrast, if miners decide to leave the network, the hashing difficulty will go down, keeping the block time constant even though there is less computational power dedicated to the network.

The process of mining requires miners to keep hashing the block header over and over again, by iterating through the nonce until one in the network miner eventually produces a valid block hash. When a valid hash is found, the founder node will broadcast the block to the network. All other nodes will check if the hash is valid and, if so, add the block into their copy of the blockchain and move on to mining the next block.

However, it sometimes happens that two miners broadcast a valid block at the same time and the network ends up with two competing blocks. Miners start to mine the next block based on the block they received first. The competition between these blocks will continue until the next block is mined based on either one of the competing blocks. The block that gets abandoned is called an orphan block or a stale block. The miners of this block will switch back to mining the chain of the winner block.

- **Mining pools:**

While the block reward is granted to the miner who discovers the valid hash first, the probability of finding the hash is equal to the portion of the total mining power on the network. Miners with a small percentage of the mining power stand a very small chance of discovering the next block on their own. Mining pools are created to solve this problem. It means pooling of resources by miners, who share their processing power over a network, to split the reward equally among everyone in the pool, according to the amount of work they contribute to the probability of finding a block.

Cryptocurrency mining really doesn't revolve around mining Bitcoin alone. It also includes other digital currencies as well, and their number is constantly growing. Apart from traditional mining approaches, you can benefit from cloud mining. Thus, there is no need to have mining equipment that you run in your facility/home, nor do you pay for electricity or deal with the noise & heat.

- **Cloud mining**

Cloud mining happens in the "cloud." That basically means that the hardware used for mining is not physically located at your premises, but it is accessed remotely through the internet. Most of the hardware, particularly for mining Bitcoins and other popular coins, is now found in specialized data centers. The goal is to facilitate transactions or generate new blocks of coins by essentially solving complex mathematical equations.

Hardware mining of cryptocurrencies requires large financial investments from a user and might be less beneficial for novice market participants. What is more, with the advent of large data centers built on the use of specialized ASIC devices, the mining process becomes less effective, even if you use powerful equipment at your home.

If you are not ready to invest a lot of money in specialized mining hardware and are looking for a different way to run the business or buy hashing power, you always have an option with such platforms as Xive– a proven cloud mining service provider. Such platforms began to gain popularity about two to three years ago and are still improving their efficiency. The cloud mining method works quite simply: instead of acquiring equipment and creating your own farms, you just buy power from a cloud mining service. The algorithm for its creation and operation is as follows:

- ☐ Miners, offering a service, buy equipment, install, and configure it (as a rule, this is a very large data center);
- ☐ They introduce all the information about the company, its technical capabilities, prices for services, and the conditions for concluding contracts;
- ☐ A user who wants to purchase part of the computing capacity registers on the marketplace, selects mining contracts, and rents these machines for a fixed fee;
- ☐ As a result of the transaction, the individual receives hashrate directly to his/her mining pool and receives payouts for contributing to the mining process.
- ☐ Today, there are many cloud mining services to choose from, and many companies are constantly opening as well. When deciding on a service to use, you should always check the company's reputation as well as the contract conditions in order to pick exactly what you need.

4. Some useful websites for cryptocurrency mining and cloud minining:

Here a list of some useful websites for crypt currencies mining and cloud mining.

Note that some of these sites may be not active and closed now. I just gave sample of the websites that worked before publishing this book.

- Cloud Mining through World Mining https://world-mining.net
- Cloud Mining through Cryptomining.Farm https://www.cryptominingfarm.io/
- Mining through Miner Gate https://minergate.com/
- Mining through faucet hub website
- Minining through Litecoinpool.org with CPU miner
- Mining through EOBOT website https://www.eobot.com
- https://ltcminer.us
- https://www.dualmine.com
- https://www.1rc.co/
- https://mining-up.com/registration
- https://dogebank.io
- https://bountyminer.io/
- https://dogebear.world/account.php
- https://coinspot.fun/cs/index.php
- Mining through Nice hash website www.nicehash.com
- Using nano mining pool to mine currency https://nanopool.org/
- Using Mining Pool Hub Using Mining Pool Hub miningpoolhub.com to mine currency.
- Mining using and CPU miner https://suprnova.cc/:
- Using Dwarfpool https://dwarfpool.com/
- Using moneropool to mine currency http://moneropool.com.
- Using Mining Pool mining-pool.info to mine currency.
- Using Nano exchange https://nanex.co
- Using Slushapool with ASIC Miner
- Mining through the coinpot.co website
- Mining through https://cointiply.com/mine
- https://www.manohash.com/
- Cloud Mining website for litcoine. It gives 25 MH/s mining power
- http://dogecoin.browserhash.com/index.php
- https://mineiota.com/
- https://dogecoins.online
- https://btconline.io/dashboard
- https://dogelands.com/index.php

- https://ethonline.io/
- https://www.cryptolux.io
- https://t.me/DOGEClick
- https://t.me/Ethereum_Hourly_bot?start=
- https://t.me/ETH_Faucet_bot?start
- https://t.me/Bitcoin_Hourly_bot
- https://dogeminers.us
- https://t.me/ETH_Mini_Mining_Bot?start
- https://t.me/btc_miner_robot
- https://t.me/telehash_bot?start
- https://liteminer.cc/index.php
- https://t.me/ETH_Miner_bot? https://dogecoins.online/ start
- https://dogecoins.online/
- https://hashtorin.net/dashboard
- https://coinmining.me
- https://hashcloud_mining_bot
- https://coinmining.me
- https://platform.jsecoin.com/

5. Airdrop and Bounty definitions:

In the cryptocurrency and blockchain ecosystem, the term "Airdrop" refers to the distribution of digital assets to the public, either by virtue of holding a certain other token or simply by virtue of being an active wallet address on a particular blockchain.

This is separate and distinct from the allocation of tokens or coins that happen via an ICO event. During ICOs, the digital asset being offered is typically purchased using an alternate coin or token. In the case of airdrops, there is no purchase required from the recipient, meaning that the assets are distributed for free.

An airdrop, in the cryptocurrency business, is a marketing stunt that involves sending free coins or tokens to wallet addresses in order to promote awareness of a new virtual currency. Small amounts of the new virtual currency are sent to wallets for free or in return for a small service such as retweeting a post sent by the company issuing the currency.

In Bounty programs, participants get cryptocurrencies in exchange for promotion. Crypto bounties are incentives paid to those who promote the initial coin offer (ICO). Participants perform various activities related to ICO. This program helps people to know about the company. People get rewards in the form of tokens. The company assigns tasks to participants. These tasks vary in their difficulty levels. These tasks can be just following the company on social sites or write a review about the product. There are two stages of bounty:

6. Some online sources to looking for airdrops events:

A bounty is a payment or reward often offered by a group as an incentive for the accomplishment of a task by someone usually not associated with the group. Bounties are most commonly issued for the capture or retrieval of a person or object

Many crypto companies distribute free coins to their communities to increase their project's visibility commonly known as "airdrops."

Most of the airdrops "bounty" drops, which will reward you with tokens for completing simple social media tasks (Joining their Telegram group, reposting on Twitter, etc.). This offering creates a win-win scenario because the company gets free marketing, and you get free crypto. Other airdrops will reward you for simply holding a specific coin without expectation of any reciprocal consideration. Airdrops is a growing trend of how crypto projects spread their tokens to as many people as possible.

Here some online sources to assist you find airdrops events:

- AirdropAlert.com
- CryptoCreed.com/airdrop
- ERC20 Airdrops – Telegram Channel
- Alertairdrop.com
- Coinairdrop.com
- Airdrop List (free token)
- Complete List of Crypto Airdrops for March 2018
- Crypto Airdrops Twitter Channel
- Airdrop Notify
- Airdrops list by Sabbir Ahmed
- Cryptocurrencytalk.com – Airdrop Thread
- AirdropAddict.com
- Airdropscouter.com
- BitcoinGarden Forum Thread
- Airdropscouter.com
- https://airdrops.club/
- https://airdrops.io/
- Airdrop Junkie – Google Spreadsheet
- https://icodrops.com/bounty-list/
- Airdrops.io
- http://coinwoot.com/airdrop
- http://dropscrypto.com/
- https://www.desiairdrops.com/
- https://twitter.com/AirdropDet
- https://t.me/myairdrop4

- http://dropscrypto.com/
- https://www.desiairdrops.com/

Here I will just mention example of announced airdrop in https://airdrops.io/insolar/

Insolar platform is designed to enable the efficient formation, management, and reconfiguration of business networks. It focuses on business needs, enables shared business processes across enterprises, is aligned with current enterprise IT practices, considers the long-term total cost of ownership goals, and is both decentralized and scalable.

Insolar is airdropping **3 XNS (~ $3)** coins each to max 3,000 participants. Participate in our exclusive airdrop by completing simple tasks and submit your details to the below form to receive your rewards. After claiming you can also invite unlimited friends using your referral link and earn **1 XNS (~ $1)** for each referral.

Step-by-Step Guide:

1.   Join Insolar Telegram group, Insolar Telegram channel and Airdrops.io Telegram channel.
2.   Do not discuss airdrop related topics in the Insolar Telegram group.
3.   Follow Insolar and Airdrops.io on Twitter.
4.   Your Twitter account must have a minimum of 10 followers.
5.   Retweet this tweet using hashtag $XNS.
6.   Visit xns.insolar.io, find out more about the project and create your wallet address.
7.   Like Insolar and Airdrops.io on Facebook. (Optional)
8.   Follow Insolar on Reddit and upvote the last 5 posts. (Optional)
9.   Follow Insolar on Instagram and like the last 5 posts. (Optional)
10.   Submit your details to the below airdrop form.
11.   You will get 3 XNS (~ $3) coins.
12.   Also get 1 XNS (~ $1) coins for each referral by inviting your friends using your referral link. Referral system is uncapped, means you can invite unlimited friends.
13.   Check your referral balance using the form below.

7. Some Youtube channels to fellow up latest airdrops, faucets and mining websites:

1- Make Money Online اربح من الانترنت

https://www.youtube.com/watch?v=QbiPGbcREWM

2- Genuine Airdrops

https://www.youtube.com/channel/UCVV0P4DJvoxvLsMY3Ygip_w

3- Genuine Airdrops : News & Updates

https://www.youtube.com/channel/UCLPpL4avILLOXh78X6mAJAQ

4- Airdrop Detective

https://www.youtube.com/watch?v=utHHrxICFko&feature=youtu.be

8. Some websites to get information about cryptocurrency prices and market capitalization

Here list of some websites that you can use to get the latest crypto currency market overview and analysis including price, market cap, trading volume, and more. There are complete crypt currency market coverage with real-time coin prices, charts and crypto market cap featuring over 7199 coins on more than 287 exchanges

- https://coinmarketcap.com/
- https://coincodex.com/
- https://cmc.io/
- https://www.coingecko.com/en

As example, here screenshot of the coins that has highest market cap in exchanges at the time I am writing this report. It can be found from https://www.coingecko.com/en/coins/all

All Cryptocurrencies
◎ Explore the crypto universe

				Market Cap		24h Volume			Price			24h Change	
USD ▾				All	⇕	All			All	⇕		All	⇕

#	Coin	Symbol	Price	1h	24h	7d	30d	24h Volume	Circulating Supply	Total Supply	Mkt Cap
1	Bitcoin	BTC	$8,718.45	2.1%	-10.7%	-2.8%	19.5%	$61,396,397,234	18,372,975	21 Million	$160,863,720,096
2	Ethereum	ETH	$188.84	1.8%	-11.3%	-11.7%	11.0%	$19,049,271,216	110,873,242	∞	$20,901,141,705
3	XRP	XRP	$0.201600	1.7%	-8.2%	-9.6%	1.8%	$3,658,287,160	44,112,853,111	100 Billion	$8,857,414,145
4	Tether	USDT	$1.01	0.8%	1.0%	0.7%	1.0%	$77,026,154,609	8,462,697,287	7.51 Billion	$8,545,649,524
5	Bitcoin Cash	BCH	$237.01	2.7%	-11.0%	-9.2%	-7.8%	$5,282,291,296	18,403,415	21 Million	$4,344,928,307
6	Bitcoin SV	BSV	$183.56	2.8%	-13.6%	-13.8%	-14.3%	$2,415,004,622	18,401,908	21 Million	$3,365,812,094
7	Litecoin	LTC	$42.18	2.1%	-12.0%	-14.3%	-9.1%	$4,600,240,130	64,700,618	84 Million	$2,725,400,243
8	EOS	EOS	$2.44	2.3%	-12.4%	-17.0%	-10.7%	$4,191,081,820	936,753,336	∞	$2,272,076,283
9	Binance Coin	BNB	$15.29	2.3%	-10.8%	-12.7%	1.7%	$431,599,274	147,883,948	180 Million	$2,247,382,298
10	Tezos	XTZ	$2.54	1.6%	-12.2%	-10.4%	20.4%	$197,430,637	709,954,095	∞	$1,798,644,266
11	Cardano	ADA	$0.04714798	2.8%	-9.1%	-7.5%	30.1%	$264,313,688	31,112,484,646	45 Billion	$1,462,223,455
12	ChainLink	LINK	$3.76	1.5%	-8.6%	-1.5%	13.7%	$679,327,031	379,509,559	1 Billion	$1,420,996,427
13	OKB	OKB	$4.89	1.6%	-8.7%	-11.7%	0.2%	$94,544,074	282,838,291	300 Million	$1,384,249,205
14	Stellar	XLM	$0.06289755	1.1%	-12.9%	-16.3%	21.4%	$676,174,552	20,232,488,961	50 Billion	$1,268,566,212
15	LEO Token	LEO	$1.10	0.6%	2.6%	1.4%	7.0%	$14,584,079	979,752,587	985 Million	$1,072,255,813
16	Crypto.com Coin	CRO	$0.06383436	1.8%	-7.1%	6.0%	28.1%	$7,484,892	16,734,703,196	100 Billion	$1,065,433,977
17	Monero	XMR	$58.82	1.1%	-8.3%	-8.8%	0.6%	$147,124,758	17,555,271	∞	$1,028,244,965
18	TRON	TRX	$0.01435045	2.0%	-12.0%	-12.2%	6.8%	$1,826,809,398	66,140,232,427	99.3 Billion	$946,131,261
19	Huobi Token	HT	$3.80	1.4%	-9.0%	-10.9%	-2.7%	$301,288,758	233,370,545	500 Million	$882,210,908
20	USD Coin	USDC	$1.00	0.3%	0.4%	0.4%	0.5%	$551,388,887	746,275,498	746 Million	$745,602,869
21	Ethereum Classic	ETC	$6.23	2.7%	-12.2%	-16.5%	5.7%	$2,637,161,598	116,319,790	211 Million	$722,474,501
22	NEO	NEO	$9.83	2.7%	-13.3%	6.7%	22.5%	$946,602,742	70,530,000	100 Million	$689,881,317
23	Dash	DASH	$72.23	2.1%	-10.2%	-13.3%	-12.0%	$844,082,170	9,454,333	18.9 Million	$680,824,531
24	IOTA	MIOTA	$0.184648	3.1%	-8.5%	-3.4%	6.4%	$18,555,611	2,779,530,283	2.78 Billion	$512,940,649
25	Cosmos	ATOM	$2.50	2.0%	-10.6%	-12.9%	-3.1%	$199,825,945	186,747,544	∞	$464,652,180
26	Zcash	ZEC	$40.86	1.9%	-10.4%	-12.1%	-0.3%	$389,456,035	9,126,519	?	$371,418,165
27	NEM	XEM	$0.03781548	1.8%	-8.0%	-12.0%	-3.8%	$27,050,125	8,999,999,999	9 Billion	$338,809,103
28	Dogecoin	DOGE	$0.00241415	2.0%	-6.0%	-4.7%	19.3%	$231,899,766	124,502,452,509	?	$299,292,389
29	Ontology	ONT	$0.469861	1.0%	-6.5%	-6.9%	4.7%	$139,964,765	637,351,170	1 Billion	$297,870,733
30	Maker	MKR	$330.57	2.0%	-4.3%	-6.4%	0.9%	$4,222,072	887,583	1.01 Million	$292,097,832
31	Basic Attention Token	BAT	$0.196107	2.7%	-12.7%	3.3%	14.5%	$157,930,989	1,460,977,137	1.5 Billion	$285,829,178
32	FTX Token	FTT	$2.73	1.1%	-11.3%	-14.7%	0.3%	$10,899,724	100,046,246	346 Million	$273,086,939
33	VeChain	VET	$0.00414755	2.3%	-10.7%	-8.0%	6.6%	$209,592,629	64,423,896,728	86.7 Billion	$266,279,477
34	Paxos Standard	PAX	$1.01	1.1%	1.3%	1.4%	1.4%	$824,328,445	249,963,920	250 Million	$252,387,830
35	DigiByte	DGB	$0.01875685	-1.3%	-16.6%	-1.0%	177.4%	$18,236,155	13,123,065,926	21 Billion	$245,767,124
36	0x	ZRX	$0.379736	3.3%	-14.3%	79.2%	101.0%	$251,527,649	653,498,325	1 Billion	$245,292,619
37	Binance USD	BUSD	$0.997380	-0.2%	-0.3%	-0.2%	-0.2%	$250,418,489	183,776,424	184 Million	$183,294,852
38	Bitcoin Gold	BTG	$8.88	2.8%	-10.5%	-12.8%	-8.8%	$39,876,831	17,513,924	21 Million	$155,003,695
39	Decred	DCR	$13.29	1.7%	-9.3%	-9.1%	4.9%	$125,419,518	11,471,334	21 Million	$151,934,661
40	Lisk	LSK	$1.08	2.0%	-11.0%	-15.6%	3.1%	$6,403,786	139,585,514	?	$149,556,074
41	Theta Network	THETA	$0.141680	1.6%	-12.9%	3.4%	63.0%	$8,984,646	1,000,000,000	1 Billion	$141,669,877
42	ICON	ICX	$0.260415	2.5%	-13.1%	-10.0%	2.8%	$39,610,222	542,363,769	800 Million	$140,940,460
43	Algorand	ALGO	$0.191582	2.2%	-13.7%	-12.6%	-4.8%	$69,187,193	737,401,318	10 Billion	$140,594,207
44	TrueUSD	TUSD	$1.01	0.6%	0.6%	0.7%	0.7%	$1,497,400,466	139,324,871	139 Million	$139,668,945
45	Numeraire	NMR	$30.19	1.6%	-13.4%	37.5%	72.7%	$1,540,038	4,635,155	11 Million	$139,447,163
46	Hedera Hashgraph	HBAR	$0.03423174	2.2%	-12.7%	-21.7%	-6.3%	$10,934,866	4,077,684,788	50 Billion	$138,909,335

9. Some trusted cryptocurrency exchanges :

A cryptocurrency exchange is any system that operates on the basis of trading cryptocurrencies with other assets. Like a traditional financial exchange, the cryptocurrency exchange's core operation is to allow for the buying and selling of these digital assets, as well as others. A cryptocurrency exchange is also known as a digital currency exchange (DCE).

You can find list of exchanges among with their ranks in any coin market caps. As example: https://www.coingecko.com/en/exchanges

Here I will just mention the most cryptocurrency exchanges that I trust them since they have lowest fees and an easy trading rules

- https://mercatox.com
- https://www.bitstamp.net/
- https://sg.upbit.com/
- https://p2pb2b.io/
- https://crex24.com/
- https://www.kucoin.com/

Here screenshot of a list of the best trusted exchanges according to coingecko.com rating. You can get the list of exchanges in market from https://www.coingecko.com/en/exchanges/

#	Exchange	Trust Score Beta	24h Volume (Normalized)	24h Volume	Visits (SimilarWeb)	# Coins	# Pairs	Last 7 Days
1	Binance (Centralized)	10	$3,272,848,770	$3,272,848,770	23,190,000	190	594	
2	OKEx (Centralized)	10	$1,295,017,845	$1,996,174,646	5,631,000	142	365	
3	Coinbase Pro (Centralized)	10	$918,850,594	$918,850,594	4,704,000	25	59	
4	Huobi Global (Centralized)	10	$730,933,967	$2,109,463,907	3,178,249	229	558	
5	Kraken (Centralized)	10	$484,749,273	$484,749,273	3,638,000	33	146	
6	Bitfinex (Centralized)	10	$460,757,027	$460,757,027	2,601,000	134	273	
7	Bitstamp (Centralized)	10	$417,873,810	$452,833,899	1,817,000	5	14	
8	Bithumb (Centralized)	10	$304,883,394	$304,883,394	3,597,000	107	108	
9	CoinTiger (Centralized)	10	$213,176,824	$261,482,734	928,157	87	142	
10	FTX (Centralized)	10	$171,771,964	$171,771,964	1,013,000	81	132	
11	bitFlyer (Centralized)	10	$143,211,233	$143,211,233	1,752,000	3	6	
12	KuCoin (Centralized)	10	$123,415,091	$123,415,091	1,104,000	202	436	
13	Poloniex (Centralized)	10	$116,281,013	$116,281,013	1,617,000	72	148	
14	Bittrex (Centralized)	10	$58,889,662	$58,889,662	2,502,000	254	414	
15	Binance US (Centralized)	10	$39,112,414	$39,112,414	323,540	30	59	
16	HitBTC (Centralized)	9	$233,429,784	$1,026,116,380	1,015,000	378	877	
17	Gate.io (Centralized)	9	$145,949,757	$145,949,757	712,094	232	448	
18	Bitbank (Centralized)	9	$72,993,140	$72,993,140	1,307,000	6	8	
19	Gemini (Centralized)	9	$64,383,917	$64,383,917	490,176	9	27	
20	AEX (Centralized)	9	$62,512,036	$80,483,550	271,815	118	145	

#	Exchange	Trust Score	24h Volume (Normalized)	24h Volume	Visits (SimilarWeb)	# Coins	# Pairs	Last 7 Days
22	OKCoin (Centralized)	9	$26,827,527	$32,645,685	110,872	16	21	
23	EXMO (Centralized)	9	$26,616,086	$26,616,086	2,982,000	45	175	
24	CEX.IO (Centralized)	9	$14,693,899	$14,693,899	721,303	23	81	
25	Bitkub (Centralized)	9	$14,393,480	$14,393,480	917,528	28	32	
26	Bitso (Centralized)	9	$14,326,051	$14,326,051	1,417,000	10	21	
27	OKEx Korea (Centralized)	9	$2,541,981	$2,541,981	21,475	69	132	
28	Float SV (Centralized)	9	$507,207	$507,207	9,072	9	16	
29	ZB (Centralized)	8	$880,485,733	$3,812,648,260	3,638,845	91	201	
30	WhiteBIT (Centralized)	8	$407,361,266	$407,361,266	3,433,000	45	137	
31	Upbit (Centralized)	8	$327,118,005	$327,118,005	2,915,000	173	263	

And here screenshot of the spot trading page at Kucoin.com exchange
https://trade.kucoin.com/spot

And here screenshot of the asset page at Kucoin.com exchange
https://www.kucoin.com/assets/main-account

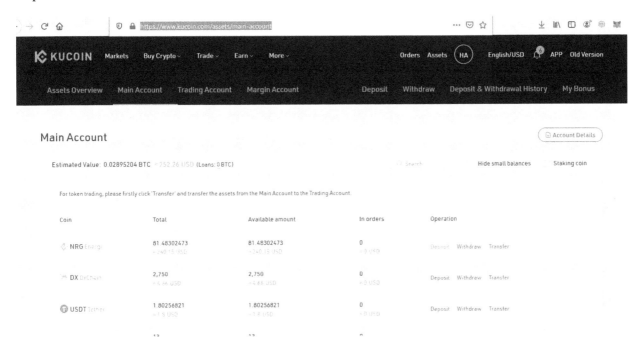

10. Some exchanger monitoring platforms

There are some websites that assist you to find favorable e-currency exchange rates on the best digital money exchangers.

1-First of all select the currency pair you'd like to trade in the table on the left (for example, choose Perfect Money EUR in the "Give" column and PayPal USD in the "Get" column).You will be forwarded to the list of exchangers offering deals in the currency pair of your choice.

2-Choose the exchanger that has the best rate and check if this provider has sufficient reserves for the chosen currency. View recent feedback left by other customers of to make sure the service provider isn't experiencing any sort of technical difficulties at the moment.

3- Click on the name of the selected exchanger. The website of the exchange provider will open in a new window.

4-Follow the instructions on the exchanger's website to complete your exchange request;

Here some websites:

- https://www.bestchange.com/
- https://www.okchanger.com/

As example, here screenshot at okchanger.com that will show the possible exchanges that can be used to transfer Eth to USD in Paypal:

https://www.okchanger.com/CRYPTOCURRENCIES-ETHEREUM-to-PAYPAL-USD

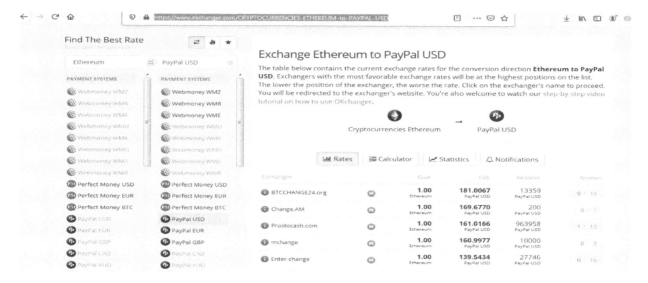

And here screenshot at bestchange.com that will show the possible exchanges that can be used to transfer Eth to USD in Paypal:

https://www.bestchange.com/ethereum-to-paypal-usd.html

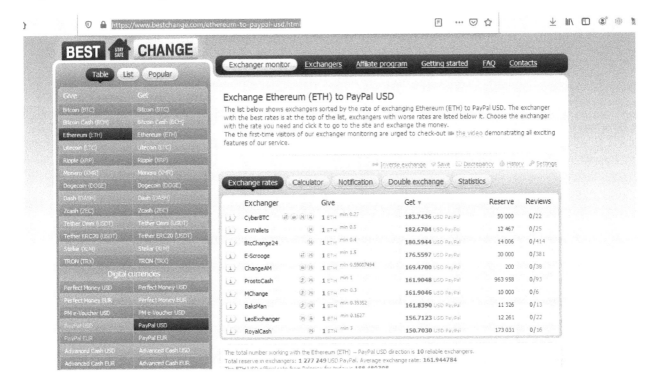

11. Some electronic currencies exchangers:

There are some On-line service designed for those who wants to exchange electronic currencies quickly, safely and at a favorable rate, such as: Webmoney, Perfect Money, AdvCash, Payeer, Skrill, Neteller, Epay, Payza, PayPal, Visa/Master Card, Western union, MoneyGram, Bitcoin, Ethereum, Litecoin.

Cheapest exchagers that I found

1) Paytiz.com - eCurrency Money Exchanger:

Our website is dedicated to those who wish to exchange own currency in a luxurious way! We welcome you on our grounds and hope that our online service will deliver you the most awesome experience you ever had. Our major point is to provide our clients the safest and quickest method to make transactions using each of the following payment systems: Visa/Master Card, Webmoney, Perfect Money, Bitcoin, Ethereum, Litecoin, Bitcoin Cash, PayPal, Payeer, AdvCash, Epay, Skrill, Neteller, AliPay, Yandex,Money, SEPA/EU Transfer, UK Faster Payment Service, WIRE.

As example, here screenshot at Paytiz.com to transfer Eth to USD at Paypal https://paytiz.com/exchange_ETH_to_PPUSD/

2) https://www.airtm.com:

Airtm is dollar wallet connected to bank and e-money networks via a peer-to-peer exchange. Users hold their funds as dollars, and can send, receive, add, and withdraw funds domestically and internationally. Airtm is used by hundreds of thousands of people throughout the world to save in dollars, send and receive money locally and abroad, and access funds in payment processors. Airtm facilitates exchanges between payment methods and dollars held in Airtm (called AirUSD) by matching you with peers moving funds in the opposite direction. This peer to peer matching is what distinguishes Airtm from other e-wallets and allows your Airtm funds to be connected to more payment methods, at better rates, throughout the world.

To add funds:

1. Go to Add/Withdraw and select the Add tab and your payment method.

2. Input the amount you would like to add to your Airtm balance, confirm payment method details and submit request.

3. Once a peer accepts your request, funds from your peer's Airtm balance are then held in escrow for you.

4. You will then transfer funds to your peer using your selected payment method.
5. Your peer will then confirm funds received, releasing escrowed funds to your Airtm balance completing the transaction.

CPSIA information can be obtained
at www.ICGtesting.com
Printed in the USA
BVHW011024061221
623327BV00016B/681